The Lazy GIANT

Ivan Jones

Illustrated by
Dee Shulman

OXFORD
UNIVERSITY PRESS

OXFORD

UNIVERSITY PRESS

Great Clarendon Street, Oxford OX2 6DP

Oxford University Press is a department of the University of Oxford.
It furthers the University's objective of excellence in research, scholarship,
and education by publishing worldwide in

Oxford   New York

Auckland   Cape Town   Dar es Salaam   Hong Kong   Karachi
Kuala Lumpur   Madrid   Melbourne   Mexico City   Nairobi
New Delhi   Shanghai   Taipei   Toronto

With offices in

Argentina   Austria   Brazil   Chile   Czech Republic   France   Greece
Guatemala   Hungary   Italy   Japan   Poland   Portugal   Singapore
South Korea   Switzerland   Thailand   Turkey   Ukraine   Vietnam

Oxford is a registered trade mark of Oxford University Press
in the UK and in certain other countries

British Library Cataloguing in Publication Data

Data available

ISBN 978-0-19-915173-8

1 3 5 7 9 10 8 6 4 2

Mixed Pack (1 of 6 different titles): ISBN 978-0-19-915168-4
Class Pack (6 copies of 6 titles): ISBN 978-0-19-915167-7

Printed in China by Imago

Contents

Chapter *1*

The Giant

Once there was a horrible old Giant.
He lived in a big castle on top of a
mountain and he was very lazy.

The Giant was so lazy, he needed
servants to look after him.

But nobody wanted to work for him
at all.

One day, the Giant went down the mountain. At the bottom, was a little cottage. Twelve children lived there, all on their own.

The girls were called –

Lotty,   Dotty   and   Totty

and Bessie,   Jessie   and   Nessie.

And the boys were called –

Cliff,   Riff   and   Sniff

and Ken,   Ben   and   Den.

"Now they would make good servants," thought the Giant. So he carried them off, back to his castle.

Chapter 2

"Is my Breakfast Ready?"

Every morning, the children had to get up very early, light the big stove and fetch lots of water. Then they had to make a huge pot of porridge for the Giant.

At six o'clock, the Giant would yell,

IS MY BREAKFAST READY?

But one morning, the children woke up a bit late.

The stove wouldn't light and the water wouldn't flow. So the Giant's porridge was lumpy.

"YOU LAZY LOT!" roared the Giant.
All the children started to shake,
The castle itself began to quake!

The Giant was so angry,
he picked up Totty and
dropped her into his
bowl of porridge.

Now Totty was the smallest child of all.
She was only as tall as the Giant's boot.
Her little yellow hat fell off and bobbed
on top of the porridge.

"Yuk! Yuk! Yuk!" cried Totty.

"I may be teeny,

But I do not scream,

Not even for a giant so mean!"

As soon as the Giant's back was turned,
Lotty and Dotty pulled Totty out. Without
her hat, she looked smaller than ever.

Chapter *3*

"Is my Castle Clean?"

Every afternoon the children had to
polish and rub, sweep and scrub.
And everything had to shine
like a new pin.

At two o'clock, the Giant would yell,

IS MY CASTLE CLEAN?

But one afternoon, the polish ran out.

The head fell off the broom and the bristles fell out of the great scrubbing brush.

And the Giant found some cobwebs in a corner.

"YOU DIRTY DOPES!" boomed the Giant.

All the children started to shake,
The castle itself began to quake!

The Giant was so angry
that he picked up
Nessie and dropped
her into the waste
paper basket.

Now Nessie was the
untidiest of all the
children. She always
left things on
the floor and
forgot to comb
her hair.

"Ugh!" she
cried. "I'm in
a stew!

There's rubbish all over me,
What can I do?"

Just as soon as the Giant's back was
turned, Bessie and Jessie pulled
Nessie out.

Poor Nessie! She looked untidier
than ever!

Every night, the children had to warm
the Giant's bed with a big hot water
bottle. And the sheets had to be clean
and smooth.

At ten o'clock, the Giant would growl,

IS MY BED READY?

But one night, the hot water bottle had a hole in it. Water ran onto the bed. And the Giant found the sheets were cold and damp.

"YOU DOZY DRIPS!" roared the
Giant.

All the children started to shake,
The castle itself began to quake!

The Giant was so angry that he picked
up Sniff and dropped him in the wash-
basin. It was huge!

Now Sniff always had a cold. But he
never moaned. He was always cheerful.

"Help!" he cried.

"This basin's like an ocean!

It has a very choppy motion.

The water's rough and dirty brown.
Get me out, before I drown!"

As soon as the
Giant's back was
turned, Riff and Cliff
fished out Sniff.
After his swim in
the Giant's
basin, Sniff
sniffed
worse
than ever.

Chapter **4**

"Hurry Up!"

Every Sunday, the children had to get the
Giant's carriage ready. They had to pull it
up and down the mountain.

He would lie on soft cushions inside it.

At eleven o'clock,
the Giant would roar,

"WHERE IS MY CARRIAGE?"

But one Sunday, it rained
and rained. The lane was
muddy and the wheels were
wobbly. And so the Giant
wasn't going as fast as he liked.
He roared.

*All the children
started to shake,
 The carriage itself
began to quake!*

The Giant was so
angry that he reached
out of the window
and gave Den
a push.

Now Den was the strongest of all the children. He rolled and rolled until he was out of sight.

When the other children saw what the Giant had done, they were very upset. But they pulled the carriage to the top of the mountain.

Then

Lotty whispered to Dotty and Totty,

Totty whispered to Bessie,

Bessie whispered to Jessie and Nessie,

Nessie whispered to Cliff,

Cliff whispered to Riff and Sniff and

Sniff whispered to Ben and Ken.

They all nodded.

The children gave the carriage a huge PUSH!!!

The carriage raced down the hill.

It creaked and rattled.

It banged and clattered.

RATTLE

BANG

CLATTER

The Giant bounced
out of the carriage!
He rolled down
the mountain
until …

He fell into a
muddy hole.

Chapter 5

Just in Time

The Giant was very angry.

"YOU NINCOMPOOPS!" he roared.

GET ME OUT!

But the children were safely
out of the Giant's reach.

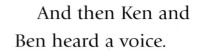

And then Ken and
Ben heard a voice.

"Help!" it said.
"Den I was and Den I am.
I thought I'd never see
you again.
But thanks
to the tree
on the side
of the hill, your
strongest friend is
with you still!"

Den was hanging
on a tree branch.

As quickly as they could, the children rescued him. They were only just in time!

GET ME OUT OF HERE!

The Giant was bellowing and banging, yelling and thumping. He made so much noise, the rocks on the mountain began to tumble.

Before the Giant could say, "YOU
BLOCKHEADS!", a big rock rolled down
the mountain and clonked him on
the head. He was knocked
out cold!

Quick as a wink, the children ran
down the mountainside, laughing
and shouting. They were
so happy to go back
home again.

As for the Giant, he got himself out of the hole and crawled back to his castle.

He never tried to catch the children again. And so, if ever he wanted anything done, he had to do it – himself!

About the author

When I was growing up I was told legends about giants. I also read *Jack the Giant Killer* stories. Later on, I read Oscar Wilde's wonderful tale, *The Selfish Giant*. I thought I'd like to write my own giant stories. I wanted them to be funny and scary and I wanted them to say something – a sort of message.